Mighty Dinosaurs

Written by Judith Simpson

TIME
LIFE
BOOKS

**The Nature Company Young Discoveries Library
is published by Time-Life Books.**

Conceived and produced by
Weldon Owen Pty Limited
43 Victoria Street, McMahons Point,
NSW, 2060, Australia
A member of the
Weldon Owen Group of Companies
Sydney • San Francisco
Copyright 1996 © US Weldon Owen Inc.
Copyright 1996 © Weldon Owen Pty Limited
Reprinted in 1997

THE NATURE COMPANY
Priscilla Wrubel, Ed Strobin, Steve Manning,
Georganne Papac, Tracy Fortini

TIME-LIFE BOOKS
Time-Life Books is a division of Time Life Inc.
Time-Life is a trademark of Time Warner Inc. U.S.A.

Vice President and Publisher: Terry Newell
Managing Editor: Donia A. Steele
Director of New Product Development: Quentin McAndrew
Vice President of Sales and Marketing: Neil Levin
Director of Financial Operations: J. Brian Birky

WELDON OWEN Pty Limited
President: John Owen
Publisher: Sheena Coupe
Associate Publisher: Lynn Humphries
Managing Editor: Rosemary McDonald
Project Editor: Jenni Bruce
Text Editor: Claire Craig
Art Director: Sue Burk
Designer: Robyn Latimer
Production Manager: Caroline Webber
Production Assistant: Kylie Lawson
Vice President, International Sales: Stuart Laurence
Coeditions Director: Derek Barton
Subject Consultants: Dr. David Kirshner,
Dr. Paul Willis

Library of Congress
Cataloging-in-Publication Data
Mighty dinosaurs / Judith Simpson.
      p. cm. -- (Young discoveries)

   ISBN 0-7835-4837-0

   1. Dinosaurs--Juvenile literature. [1. Dinosaurs.]
I. Title. II. Series.
QE862.D5S515   1996
567.9' 1--dc20   96-15737

Contents

The Age of Dinosaurs

▲ Dinosaurs came in different shapes and sizes. Some had very large bodies and tiny heads.

Dinosaurs roamed the Earth millions of years ago. Dinosaur means "terrible lizard" and, like lizards, dinosaurs were reptiles. We know a lot about dinosaurs from their remains, which we have found buried in rocks and beneath sand. Dinosaurs had scaly skin and laid eggs. Some walked on two legs, others moved on all four. Dinosaurs fed on different things—some ate only plants, the rest ate meat and hunted for their food.

▼ Some dinosaurs had spikes or bumps on their backs. Others had horns or crests on their heads. Their skin was thick and rough.

5

Meat Eaters

▲ *Oviraptor* ate eggs and could break eggshells easily with its strong beak.

Meat-eating dinosaurs had good eyesight and a strong sense of smell. They had much larger brains than plant-eating dinosaurs, so they could plan attacks to catch their prey. Some meat eaters lived on eggs, insects, lizards, small furry animals, and fish. Others gathered in packs to kill dinosaurs that were much bigger than themselves. *Tyrannosaurus* was three times as tall as a man and was one of the largest meat-eating dinosaurs.

◄ *Compsognathus* used its hands to catch prey and lift it to its mouth.

▲ *Baryonyx* used the large hooklike claw on each hand to spear fish.

Teeth as sharp as knives

When dinosaurs' teeth wore out, they grew new ones.

▶ Scientists believe that *Tyrannosaurus* used its short forelegs to hold food and to help it raise its heavy body from the ground after resting.

Plant Eaters

Not all dinosaurs were fierce hunters. Some ate only plants. For most of the age of dinosaurs, the weather was warm and wet. Plants grew easily and there were lots to choose from. Plant-eating dinosaurs needed large amounts of food to give them energy. Some roamed the land grazing on low-growing ferns. Others had long necks and, like giraffes, could stretch up to reach leaves from the tops of the tallest trees.

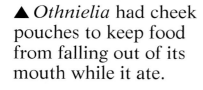

▲ *Othnielia* had cheek pouches to keep food from falling out of its mouth while it ate.

◀ Dinosaurs munched pine needles and enormous ferns. When flowering plants began to grow, at the end of the age of dinosaurs, plant eaters ate them too.

8

Stones in the stomach crushed up food

Dinosaurs never ate grass because the first grasses grew long after dinosaurs died out.

◄ *Saltasaurus* stood on its hind legs to nip leaves off trees. It had no chewing teeth so it swallowed stones to help crush the food in its stomach.

▲ *Tuojiangosaurus* had four sharp spikes on its tail to defend itself against attackers.

Styracosaurus's *frill may have changed color when it was trying to attract a mate.*

─ MIGHTY DINOSAURS ─

Spiky Dinosaurs

Some plant-eating dinosaurs had spikes on their tails and bodies, and horns on their heads. They spent most of the day quietly munching ferns or stripping leaves from trees. When they were attacked by meat-eating dinosaurs, they could not move quickly enough to escape. They used their spikes and horns to rip the bodies of their attackers. Sometimes spiky dinosaurs also fought each other over mates and feeding areas.

▼ Bony plates covered *Tuojiangosaurus's* neck, back, and tail.

▼ *Styracosaurus* looked fierce but ate only plants. Its spiky frill stopped meat eaters from pouncing on its neck.

Large and Little

This dinosaur

The giants of the dinosaur world had long necks, long tails, small heads, bodies shaped like barrels, and thick legs. *Brachiosaurus* weighed as much as 12 African elephants. *Mamenchisaurus* had a neck as long as the rest of its body. These great creatures had long tails to balance their necks. Not all dinosaurs were huge. Some were light and little. One of the smallest, *Compsognathus,* was no bigger than a pet cat or a chicken.

Dinosaurs went on growing bigger until the day they died.

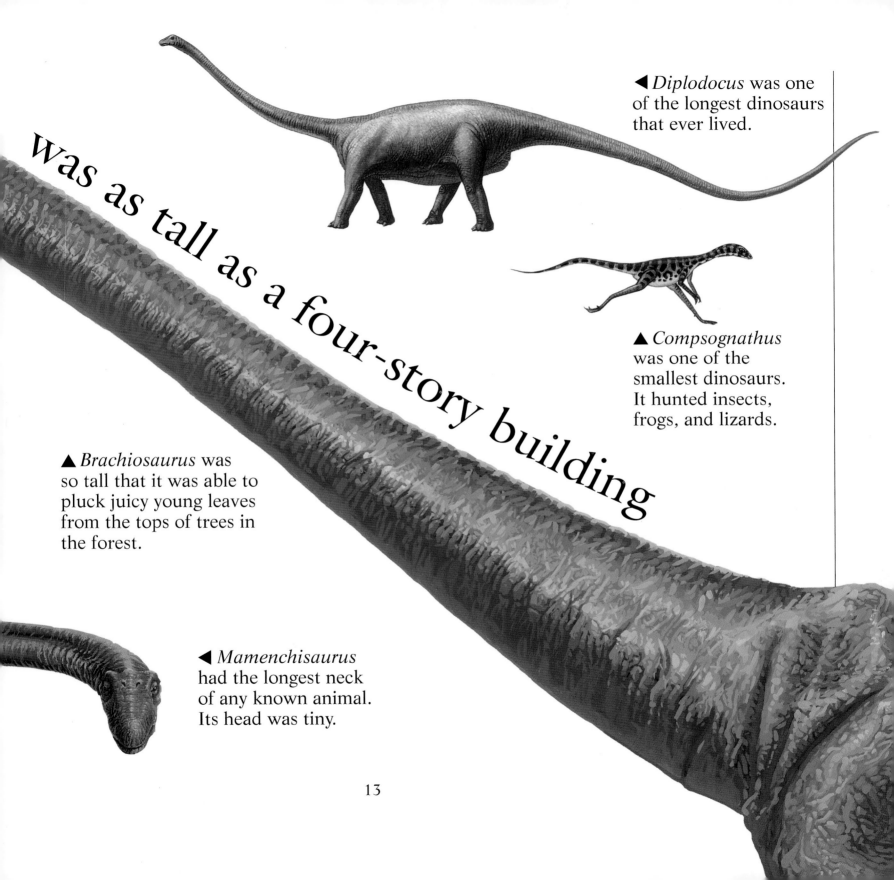

◀ *Diplodocus* was one of the longest dinosaurs that ever lived.

was as tall as a four-story building

▲ *Compsognathus* was one of the smallest dinosaurs. It hunted insects, frogs, and lizards.

▲ *Brachiosaurus* was so tall that it was able to pluck juicy young leaves from the tops of trees in the forest.

◀ *Mamenchisaurus* had the longest neck of any known animal. Its head was tiny.

13

Fast and Slow

▲ Heavy *Stegosaurus* moved more slowly than many other dinosaurs.

Most meat-eating dinosaurs moved swiftly on two legs with their tails held out behind them for balance. *Struthiomimus* ran faster than a galloping horse. Some plant eaters were small and could also run quickly, but others were very heavy and plodded slowly on four legs. Instead of running away from their enemies, they defended themselves with horns, spikes, or tails. Many stayed together in herds because they were safer in a group.

Struthiomimus *could move ten times faster than* Apatosaurus.

▶ This dinosaur looked something like an ostrich and was called *Struthiomimus,* meaning "ostrich mimic."

▶ Huge *Apatosaurus* carried its great weight on four thick legs. Smaller, lighter *Ornitholestes* dashed about on two slender legs, chasing after little lizards.

14

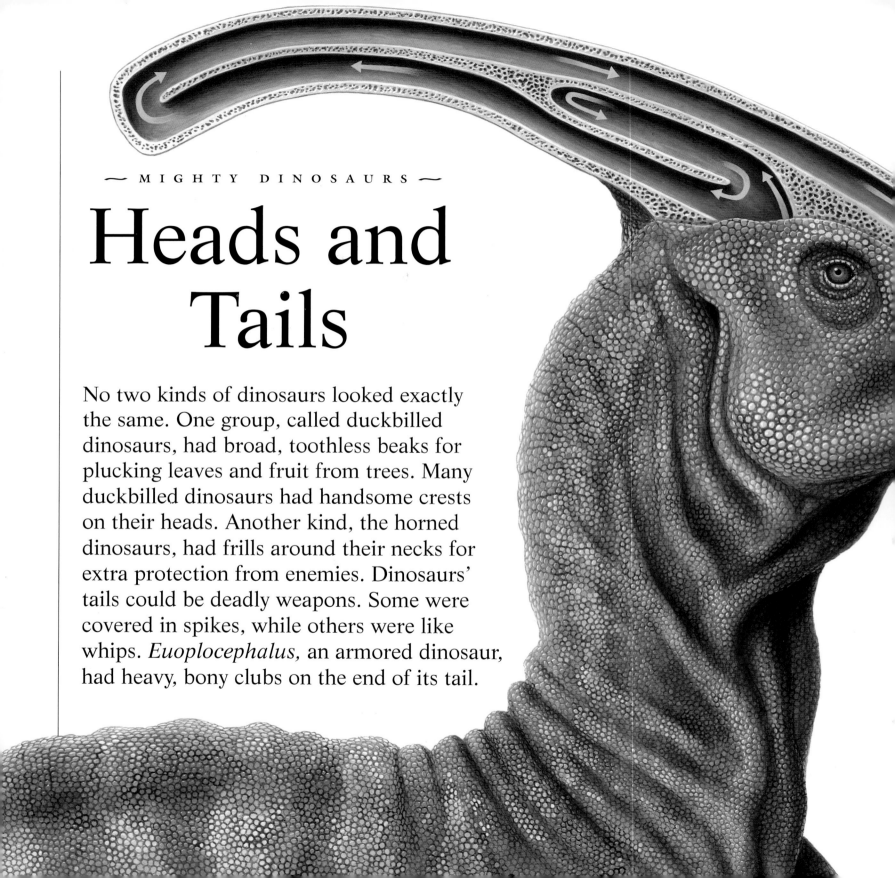

Heads and Tails

No two kinds of dinosaurs looked exactly the same. One group, called duckbilled dinosaurs, had broad, toothless beaks for plucking leaves and fruit from trees. Many duckbilled dinosaurs had handsome crests on their heads. Another kind, the horned dinosaurs, had frills around their necks for extra protection from enemies. Dinosaurs' tails could be deadly weapons. Some were covered in spikes, while others were like whips. *Euoplocephalus,* an armored dinosaur, had heavy, bony clubs on the end of its tail.

◀ Some male duckbilled dinosaurs could hoot by forcing air from their mouths through the tubes of their hollow crests, a little like blowing a trombone.

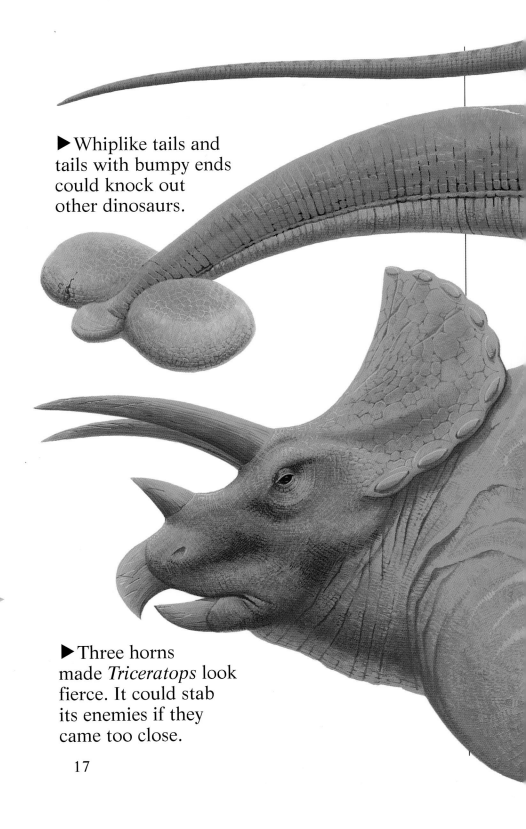

▶ Whiplike tails and tails with bumpy ends could knock out other dinosaurs.

Some armored dinosaurs even had bony eyelids.

▶ Three horns made *Triceratops* look fierce. It could stab its enemies if they came too close.

Dinosaur Babies

Dinosaur babies hatched from eggs laid in nests on the ground. These nests were made from scooped out earth or sand. The mother heated the eggs under her body or left them to warm in the sun or in rotting leaves. Dinosaur eggs were very small compared with the size of the parents. This meant that dinosaurs could lay many eggs. The more eggs they laid, the greater chance there was that some would escape from egg-thieving creatures.

▶ Some newly hatched dinosaurs were strong enough to leave the nest at once. Others had to stay to be fed by their parents.

◀ This dinosaur is a *Maiasaura,* which means "good mother lizard." She is guarding her eggs from nest robbers that might eat them.

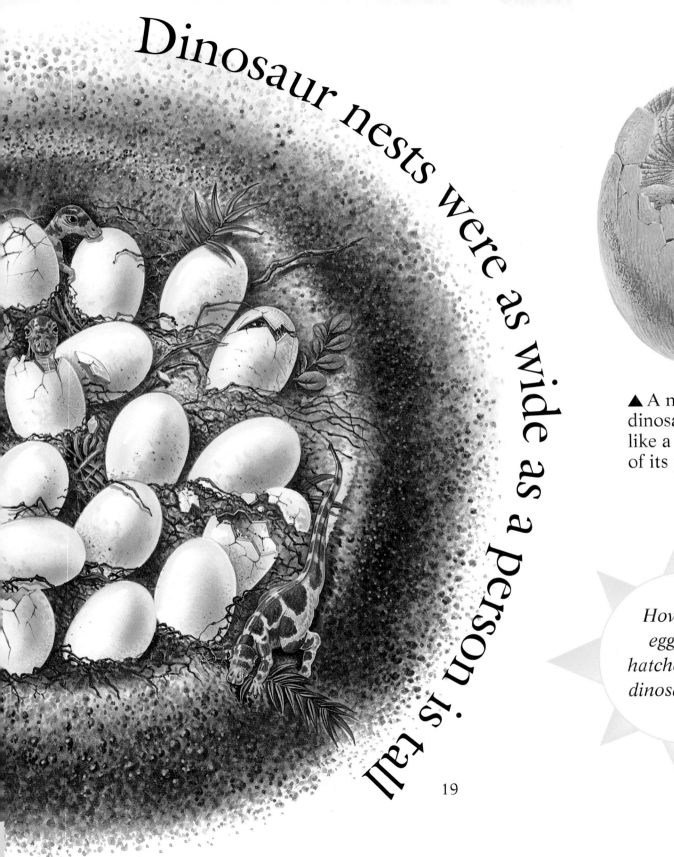

Dinosaur nests were as wide as a person is tall

19

▲ A newly hatched dinosaur looked like a small copy of its parents.

How many eggs have hatched in this dinosaur nest?

Allosaurus had a huge head and a larger brain than many other dinosaurs.

Allosaurus had hinged jaws. It could swallow large pieces of meat in one gulp.

Skeletons and Skulls

Dinosaurs' bones, teeth, and claws have been in the ground for so long that they have turned to stone and become fossils. Many are in broken pieces. Scientists can put fossils together to show what a dinosaur looked like when it was alive. Fossil bones tell us how a dinosaur moved. Fossil claws tell us how it hunted. Fossil teeth tell us what it ate. Space inside the skull tells us the size of its brain.

Many bones join to

▼ We know from its bones that *Camarasaurus* carried its weight on four thick legs that ended in strong, clawed toes. It had leaf-stripping teeth and a tiny brain.

make a dinosaur's skeleton

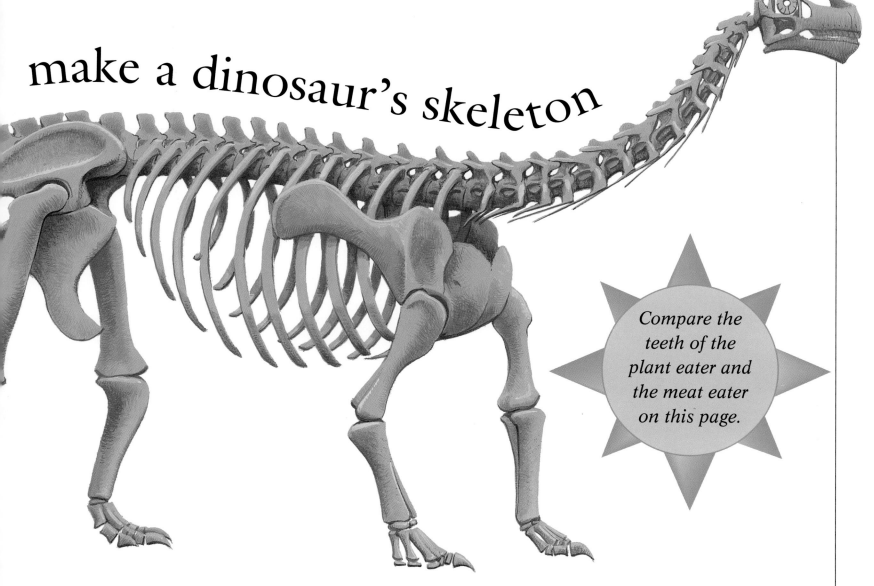

Compare the teeth of the plant eater and the meat eater on this page.

Look Inside

Fossil remains of dinosaurs are clues to how their insides worked. Like all other animals, dinosaurs had lungs, hearts, livers, stomachs, kidneys, and intestines. *Apatosaurus* and other plant-eating dinosaurs had larger stomachs than meat eaters because they digested their food more slowly. The model of *Baryonyx* on this page shows the strong muscles that covered its ribs. These helped *Baryonyx* twist its body. The muscles joined to its claws gave it a powerful grip for clutching slippery fish.

▶ *Apatosaurus* had powerful neck muscles to push leaves and twigs down into its stomach, where they were ground into a paste to make them easy to digest.

▲ *Baryonyx* used its long tail for balance when it reached into the water to snatch fish.

22

▲ *Baryonyx* had many more teeth than we do. There were 64 sharp teeth in its lower jaw.

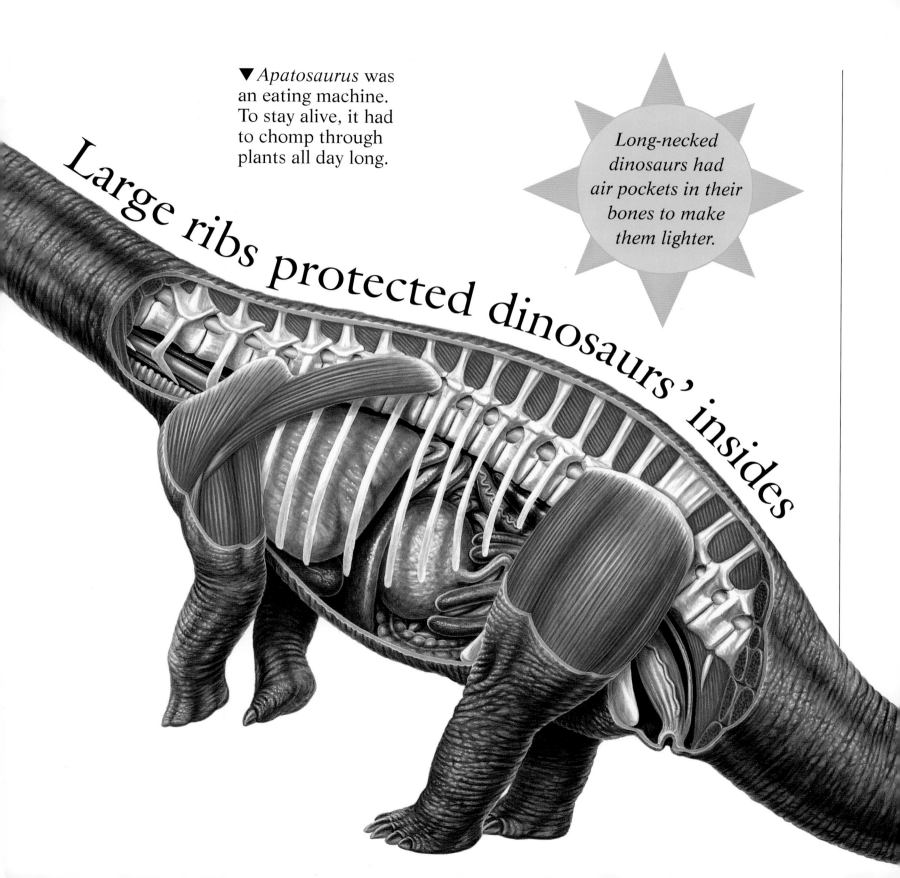

▼ *Apatosaurus* was an eating machine. To stay alive, it had to chomp through plants all day long.

Long-necked dinosaurs had air pockets in their bones to make them lighter.

Large ribs protected dinosaurs' insides

◀ This toothless pterosaur called *Pteranodon* scooped up fish in its narrow beak.

Flying and Swimming

Dinosaurs shared the Earth with other kinds of reptiles. Flying reptiles called pterosaurs glided through the skies on wings made of skin. Pterosaurs were not birds, although they looked a bit like them. Many different kinds of marine reptiles lived in the ocean. Some, such as *Peloneustes,* stayed in the water all the time. The giant turtle *Archelon* came ashore to lay its eggs. *Nothosaurus* was at home on land and in the sea.

Pterosaurs and marine reptiles were only distant cousins of the dinosaurs.

24

Small pterosaurs

▶ *Peloneustes* (top), *Archelon* (middle), and *Nothosaurus* (bottom) were all marine reptiles. *Archelon,* the largest turtle that ever lived, was the size of a car.

▼ *Rhamphorhynchus,* another kind of pterosaur, lived on fish. It had long, sharp teeth and claws on its wings.

flew like bats

Where Did They Go?

Dinosaurs disappeared about 65 million years ago. What killed them? Why did pterosaurs and many marine reptiles vanish at the same time? Perhaps rising seas flooded the land where dinosaurs lived. Perhaps they died because the Earth began to have hot and cold seasons instead of always being warm. Perhaps a giant meteorite hit the Earth and dust blotted out the sun for a while. Nobody knows for sure what caused so many animals to die out.

▼ The hot sun has begun to dry the body of this dead *Camptosaurus.* If river mud covers it, the bones will gradually turn to stone and become fossils.

Becoming a fossil takes

Most other animals disappeared at the same time as the dinosaurs.

many millions of years

▶ *Tyrannosaurus,* king of the meat eaters, was one of the last dinosaurs on Earth.

Who Survived?

The puzzle of the disappearing dinosaurs is all the more mysterious because a few animals from that time survived. Among them were turtles, crocodiles, small land reptiles, and furry, ratlike creatures. The tuatara, an unusual reptile that now lives only in New Zealand, has changed little in 240 million years. A feathered dinosaur called *Archaeopteryx* died out during the age of dinosaurs. Many scientists believe that it was the first bird and led to the birds of today.

▼ Tuataras live in burrows, but spend many daylight hours basking in the sun. At night, they look for food such as earthworms, snails, insects, and baby birds.

Tuataras

◄ *Archaeopteryx* could not fly nearly as well as birds do today.

28

▶ Crocodiles have hardly changed since the age of dinosaurs.

Archaeopteryx *used the claws on its wings to cling onto trees.*

lived at the same time as dinosaurs

Who's Who?

The age of dinosaurs lasted for more than 150 million years. These are some of the hundreds of different types that lived all over the world during that long period. Not all groups of dinosaurs were alive at the same time or in the same place. *Deinonychus* hunted animals across what is now North America when *Ouranosaurus* grazed on plants in Africa. *Hypsilophodon* wandered around the United Kingdom long before heavy, horned *Triceratops* lumbered through North America.

A dinosaur's name tells us something about the animal.

▶ *Deinonychus*
Die-non-i-kus
"Terrible claw"

▶ *Stegosaurus*
Steg-oh-sore-us
"Roof lizard"

▶ *Euoplocephalus*
You-op-loh-seff-a-lus
"True plated head"

▶ *Saltasaurus*
Salt-a-sore-us
"Lizard from Salta"

▶ *Pachycephalosaurus*
Pack-ee-seff-ah-low-sore-us
"Thick-headed lizard"

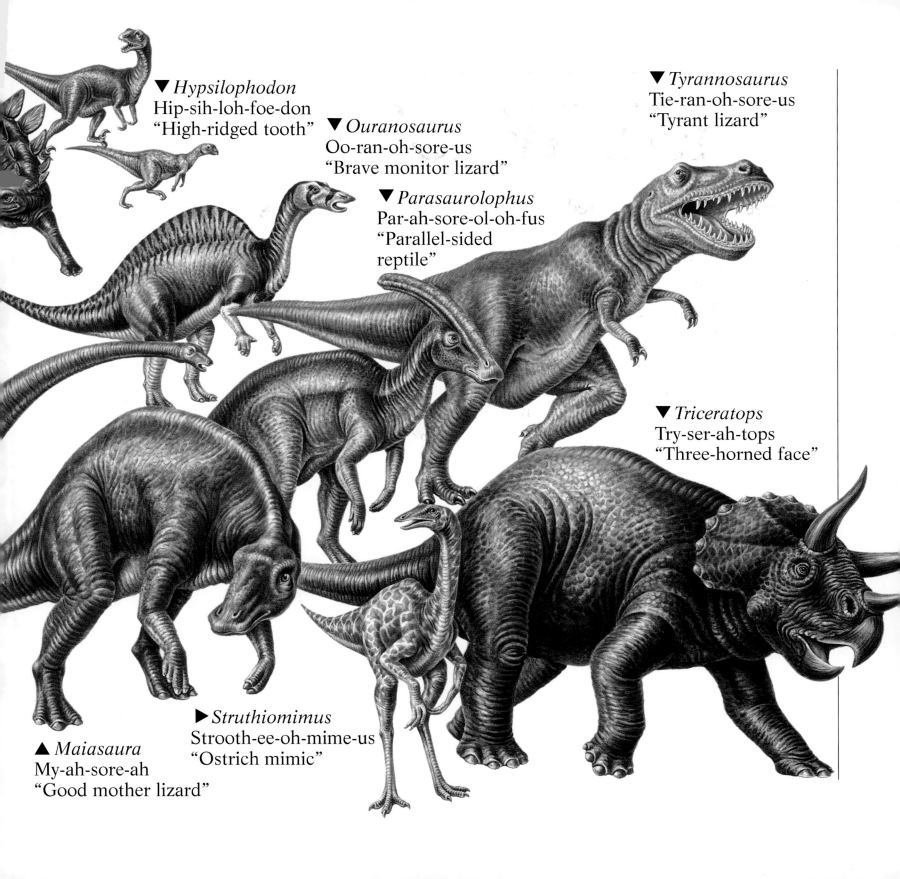

▼ *Hypsilophodon*
Hip-sih-loh-foe-don
"High-ridged tooth"

▼ *Ouranosaurus*
Oo-ran-oh-sore-us
"Brave monitor lizard"

▼ *Parasaurolophus*
Par-ah-sore-ol-oh-fus
"Parallel-sided
reptile"

▼ *Tyrannosaurus*
Tie-ran-oh-sore-us
"Tyrant lizard"

▼ *Triceratops*
Try-ser-ah-tops
"Three-horned face"

▶ *Struthiomimus*
Strooth-ee-oh-mime-us
"Ostrich mimic"

▲ *Maiasaura*
My-ah-sore-ah
"Good mother lizard"

Other titles in the series:

ANIMAL BABIES
INCREDIBLE CREATURES
SCALY THINGS
THINGS WITH WINGS
UNDERWATER ANIMALS

Acknowledgments

(t=top, b=bottom, l=left, r=right, c=center, F=front cover, B=back cover)

Simone End, Fb, Ftr, 3tr, 8bl, 10br, 14tl, 28bl, 30/31cr.
Christer Eriksson, 3bl, 7c, 11c, 29tr. **David Kirshner,** 9c,
16/17c, 20tl, 22b, 22/23c. **Frank Knight,** 10tl, 17r, 20tr, 20/21c,
25tr. **James McKinnon,** B, 12/13b, 12/13c, 15c, 19tr, 26/27c,
27tr, 28/29bc. **Colin Newman/Bernard Thornton Artists, UK,**
18bl, 18/19c, 24tl, 24/25br, 32. **Peter Schouten,** 1, 2, 4t, 4/5b,
6tl, 6bl, 6bc, 8tl, 13tr, 13cr, 14b.